Vroom!

HOT CARS

TESLA
MODEL S

JULIO DIAZ

rourkeeducationalmedia.com

*Scan for Related Titles and
Teacher Resources*

TABLE OF CONTENTS

A Car Like No Other

Cars can't think—at least not yet. If they could, however, Tesla's Model S could not be blamed for thinking it is the coolest car ever.

The Model S zooms silently down the highway. It can weave in and out of traffic effortlessly. As for looks, it turns heads wherever it goes. Best of all, it never has to go to a gas station. That's because the Model S runs on electricity. All you do is plug it in!

"The Model S got its roots from the idea of being not only the best electric car, but the best performance sedan in the marketplace" —Franz von Holzhausen, designer of the Model S

LOW AND SLEEK

Some modern all-electric cars look short and boxy, but the Tesla Model S is low and sleek. It is designed to be **aerodynamic**—allowing air to flow around it with less resistance. That enables the Model S to move faster and more smoothly and efficiently on the road.

non-framed windows contribute to clean overall look

flush door handles promote a smooth luxury feel

The Model S has **retractable** door handles that slide out when you come near to the car!

smooth flow-over hood, windshield, and roof provide excellent aerodynamics

sla Model S has a number of
hroughout the car.

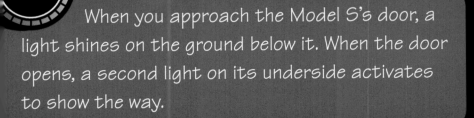

When you approach the Model S's door, a
light shines on the ground below it. When the door
opens, a second light on its underside activates
to show the way.

ALL LIT UP

The Model S looks cool during the day, but at night it's on fire with LEDs (Light **Emitting** Diodes). LEDs are cool to the touch and use considerably less power than **incandescent** bulbs. High-Intensity Discharge (HID) Xenon headlights are standard equipment on every Model S. The headlights use xenon, a gas, to provide bright, intense light on the road.

The images of the car in the controls screen match the car's actual color, its tire size, and rims. If a light is on, it lights up on the car's image as well.

The Model S is the first car to provide a full web browser **accessible** even when the car is in motion.

GET IN TOUCH

When you open the door of the Model S, you might think for a moment that you are Captain Kirk of the *Starship Enterprise*. At the center of the dashboard is a huge 17-inch (43 centimeter), high-definition touch screen. It's like an iPad, except it's bigger and easier to use. The Model S is often called "a computer on wheels." All you need to do is tap an **icon** to access everything in the car, from driving settings to power use.

NOT YOUR GRANDDAD'S BATTERY

Of course the core of the Model S is not its lights or its space-age computer system. It is the car's remarkable battery pack. The flat battery pack lies under the car floor attached to the electric drivetrain. That gives the Model S a low center of gravity, making it difficult for the car to roll over and safer in an accident. Model S has a five-star safety rating from the U.S. government, the highest awarded. Model S is available in a number of versions, so customers can choose the car that is right for them. Model S can travel 270 or more miles (434.5 kilometers) on one charge, depending on its battery pack.

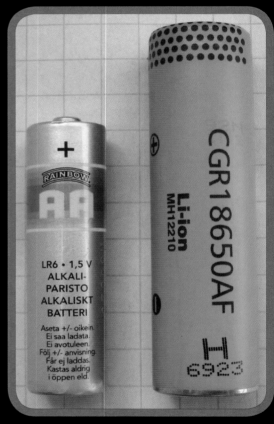

Lithium-ion batteries are rechargeable and are now widely used in cell phones, portable computers, and other consumer electronics as well as electric cars.

The flat battery pack lies under the car floor and can be easily removed and replaced. It comes in two versions: a 60 LC kilowatt pack with a range of 208 miles (335 kilometers) before recharging and an 85 LC kilowatt battery pack with a range of 265 miles (426.5 kilometers).

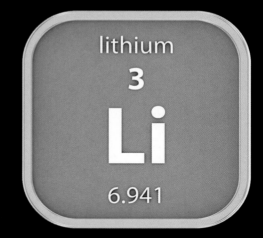

lithium

3

Li

6.941

Lithium is a soft, silver-white metal. It is present in ocean water and in some minerals.

The Model S battery pack includes a number of safety features. These include its own heating and cooling system, a smoke detection system, and a system to disconnect the battery in case of a serious accident.

Tesla Model S has a hidden charge port behind the left rear side taillight. The port is opened from within the car at the touch screen, or by depressing the button on the charge connector.

ALL CHARGED UP

If you own a Tesla, you will never have to go to a gas station again. Every Tesla comes with a mobile connector. The connector has an 18 foot (5.4 meter) cord, so it can reach just about any outlet in a garage or charging station.

There are more than 3,000 Superchargers worldwide in a network that covers North America, Europe and Asia Pacific. Using a Supercharger is free for life for all Tesla owners. It's like getting free gas!

Tesla plans to make as many Supercharger stations as possible powered by solar energy.

ON THE MOVE

If you've seen the engine of a regular gasoline or **hybrid** car, you will be surprised when you see the powertrain of a Tesla Model S. Tesla designed the Model S motor to have ONE moving part intended to last the life of the car. With two motors, one in the front and one in the rear, the car has superior traction on the road. The motors also allow the Model S to go from 0 to 60 miles (96.6 kilometers) per hour in only 2.8 seconds!

The entire Model S powertrain takes up less space than an automatic transmission! It is located above the rear trunk area.

Tesla's electric motor is now designed to last for 200,000 miles (321,869 kilometers). The company is designing a new motor that is designed to last one million miles (1,609,344 kilometers)!

PUTTING IT
TOGETHER

Building each Model S requires a number of steps in Tesla's Fremont, California, factory.

1. Metal Stamping: The Model S frame starts with uncoiled sheets of aluminum cut into rectangles called blanks. The blanks go into a press line where they are into various shapes that will eventually become hoods doors and other parts. Tesla's press line is seven stories t is the largest press in North America.

2. Body Framing: The underbody of the car is assem first. It becomes the frame for the rest of the car's bod Robots pick up the side structure and weld it to the bo structure. Then they attach the rest of the frame's stru

Robots join parts using these methods: industrial-strength adhesive bonding, various types of welding, and riveting.

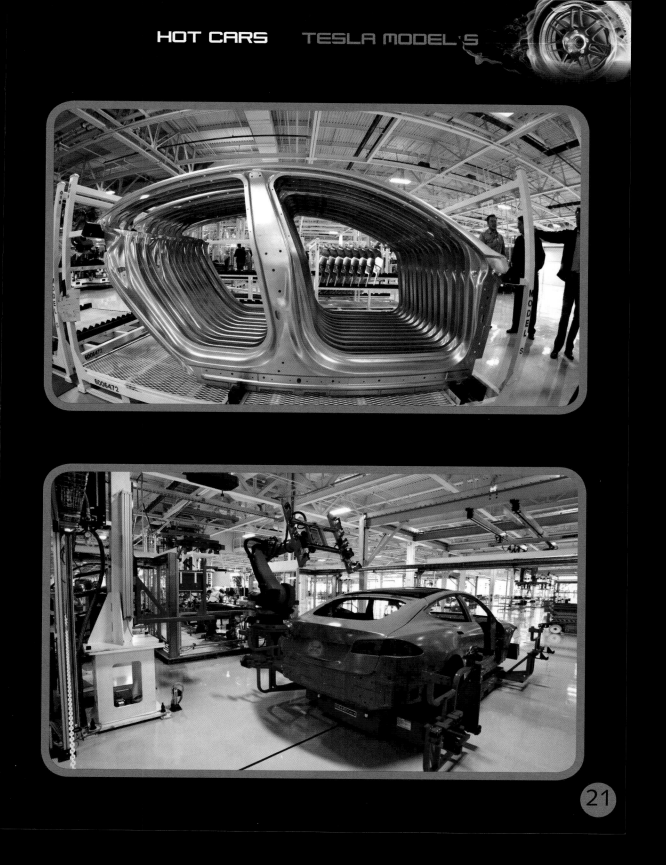

Once the car's frame is finished, lasers measure keyholes and gaps to 0.1 millimeters to ensure the assembly meets quality standards.

3. Paint Shop: To ensure a perfect finish, robots perform the entire paint process. After the paint is dry, workers wet sand the car by hand. Painting a Model S takes a day and a half.

4. Final Assembly: The frame now moves on to final assembly, where the car is put together by both workers and robots. All the **components** that make the Model S what it is, from its electric engine to batteries to its electronic components, are added and the Model S takes shape.

5. Final Inspection: When the assembly is complete, the Model S is powered up and goes through a thorough inspection before it is shipped out.

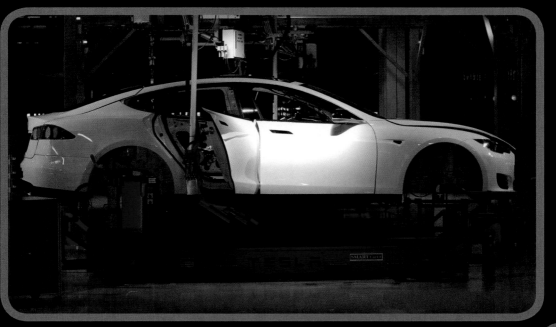

THE TESLA STORY

Tesla Motors was founded in 2003 and named after Nikola Tesla. Tesla, a scientist and electrical engineer, was a groundbreaking pioneer in developing the use of electricity.

Nikola Tesla
1856 - 1943

The company was founded by Martin Eberhard and Marc Tarpenning, who felt that the world was ready for an all-electric car that would be as fast and fun to drive as gas-powered cars. In 2004, Elon Musk, now the head of Tesla, joined the team. Tesla unveiled the Model S prototype in March 2009.

A Tesla Model S was a hit at the 2009 Frankfurt Motor Show. The show displays new cars every two years in Frankfurt am Main, Germany.

Tesla Model X at Geneva Motor Show

Tesla's cars can be purchased on the Internet instead of at car dealerships. They are built to order so customers can get exactly what they want.

The company began deliveries of the Model S in 2012. Now, the Model S is outselling every other all-electric car worldwide. Tesla will soon have two other all-electric models: Model X, an SUV, and Model 3, a less expensive version of the Model S. Tesla launched the Model X in September 2015.

Candy Apple Red Model 3 unveiled March 31, 2016

27

ELON MUSK

Elon Musk, the chief executive officer (CEO) of Tesla Motors, did not have a happy childhood. He was severely bullied, and once was thrown down a flight of stairs by a group of boys who beat him until he blacked out. He discovered computers at age 10, however, and developed a computer game at age 12. His first company, Zip2, provided online publishing software for the *New York Times* and Hearst Publishing. After selling the company to Compaq, he co-founded PayPal, then sold it to eBay. Today, Musk is "Co-founder, Chairman, CEO, and Product Architect" of Tesla Motors. A believer in clean energy, he is also chairman of SolarCity, one of the largest solar power installers in the United States. Musk's interest in space colonization led him to fund his third company, SpaceX, which designs, manufactures, and launches rockets and spacecraft. SpaceX handles cargo for the International Space Station and launches space satellites.

Elon Musk

A GREEN REVOLUTION?

Tesla's Model S and other cars embody Elon Musk's crusade to promote a pollution-free world and fight human-caused global climate change. In the United States, automobiles are the second largest source of carbon dioxide (CO_2) pollution each year. Tesla believes adoption of electric cars is crucial in reducing CO_2 emissions.

> "…Within 30 years, a majority of the new cars made in the United States will be electric. And I don't mean hybrid, I mean fully electric."
> —Elon Musk

GLOSSARY

accessible (ak-SES-uh-buhl): able to be easily accessed or reached

aerodynamic (air-oh-dye-NAM-ik): designed to move through the air very easily and quickly

components (kuhm-POH-nuhnts): parts of a larger whole, especially a machine or a system

emitting (e-MIT-ting): producing or sending out something such as heat, light, signals or sound

hybrid (HYE-brid): something that is made by combining two or more things; hybrid cars use both gasoline and electricity from a battery

icon (EYE-kahn): picture symbol on the desktop of a computer screen representing a program, function, or file

incandescent (in-kuhn-DES-uhnt): glowing with light as a result of being heated

retractable (rhee-TRAKT-uh-buhl): able to be drawn back or back in

INDEX

SHOW WHAT YOU KNOW

1. What is the main benefit of Model S's aerodynamic design?
2. Why are LED headlights better than incandescent headlights?
3. How many lithium-ion cells are contained in the Model S's battery?
4. What role do robots play in manufacturing the Model S?
5. Who was Tesla Motors named after?

WEBSITES TO VISIT

www.kids.esdb.bg/smart_inventions.html

www.TeslaMotors.com

www.conserve-energy-future.com/HowElectricCarsWork.php

ABOUT THE AUTHOR

Julio Diaz lives in California where he writes about cars and trucks. He and his family often leave the Los Angeles desert to travel and experience nature in the Mojave Desert. He doesn't own a Model S, but he would like to someday. He believes the future lies in plug-in electric cars because they are better for the environment and are already fun to drive.

Meet The Author!
www.meetREMauthors.com

www.rourkeeducationalmedia.com

PHOTO CREDITS: Cover © Taina10; pages 2-3 © CONCAVO WHEELS via Wikimedia Commons; page 4-5 © Norsk Elbilforening (Norwegian Electric Vehicle Association); pages 6-9 © Andrei Kholmov Shutterstock, inset © Taina Sohlman Shutterstock; pages 10-11 © Kaspars Grinvalds Shutterstock; page 12 © RudolfSimon, page 13 Lithium symbol © Nuno Andre Shutterstock; pages 14-15 © Taina Sohlman, inset photo © Eugene Sergeev all from Shutterstock; pages 16-17 Supercharger station © Jusdafax via Wikimedia; page 19 © Alison Cassidy; page 21 © Steve Jurvetson https://www.flickr.com/photos/jurvetson/6858564222/ , page 23 © Maurizio Pesce https://www.flickr.com/photos/; pages 24-25 Model S prototype © El monty; page 26 and 27 top © Norbert Aepli, Switzerland; page 28 Elon Musk © Steve Jurvetson https://www.flickr.com/photos/jurvetson/18659265152/; page 29 © Joseph Sohm Shutterstock; page 32 author portrait © © Yury Shchipakin, Shutterstock

Edited by: Keli Sipperley

Cover design by Rhea Magaro
Interior design by: Nicola Stratford   www.nicolastratford.com

Library of Congress PCN Data

Tesla Model S / Julio Diaz
 (*VROOM!* Hot Cars)
  ISBN 978-1-68191-749-8 (hard cover)
  ISBN 978-1-68191-850-1 (soft cover)
  ISBN 978-1-68191-941-6 (e-Book)
Library of Congress Control Number: 2016932712

Rourke Educational Media
Printed in the United States of America, North Mankato, Minnesota

Also Available as:

ROURKE'S e-Books

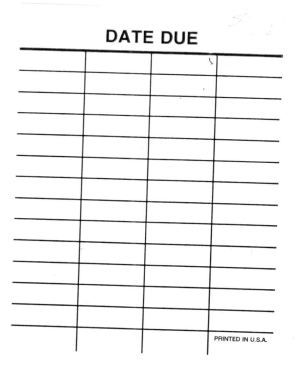

DATE DUE

PRINTED IN U.S.A.